SEPARATIONS

Moving

By Janine Amos
Illustrated by Gwen Green
Photographs by Angela Hampton

CHERRYTREE BOOKS

This book has been written to help children who are about to move home. It is also for friends of those children, to help them too.

A Cherrytree Book

Designed and produced
by A S Publishing

First published 1998
by Cherrytree Press Ltd
327 High St
Slough
Berkshire SL1 1TX

British Library Cataloguing in Publication Data
Amos, Janine
　　　Moving. - (Separations)
　　　1.Moving, Household - Juvenile literature
　　　2.Moving, Household - Psychological aspects -
Juvenile literature
　　　I.Title
　　　648.9
　　　ISBN 1 84234 166 9
Printed and bound in Belgium by Proost International Book Production

CONTENTS

Dear Gran

We're moving. Mum and Dad told me yesterday and we went to see the new house. I like my room there but it's much smaller than my old one. All the rooms are smaller. There was a lady there with all her furniture and curtains. She'll move out and we'll move in with our things. I'll have to go to a different school. I'll really miss my friends. And I won't be able to go to Art Club any more. I like Art Club. Everybody knows me there. No one will know me at the new place - it's miles away. We've got to go because Dad couldn't get a job round here. Mum and Dad have known for ages, but they didn't tell me. They said Kayleigh can come to stay sometimes.

I hope your leg is better.

Love Kim

Dear Kim
        What an exciting letter!
Thankyou for telling me your news
about moving. It sounds like you're
feeling a bit mixed up about it all,
half excited and half sad to be leaving?
I felt like that when I moved here.

        You're bound to miss your old friends.
You can write to them and meet up in the
holidays. Don't forget, you'll be busy
making new friends, too. I know how
much you enjoy Art Club. Are you sure
there isn't something like it in the new
place? Perhaps your mum or dad
could help you to find out.

        My leg is feeling much better now,
and the bandage is off.

        Write soon.
                Love Gran

JOE AND BINKIE

"We are moving! We are moving!" sang Joe's little sister Beth. She was jumping in and out of all the boxes in their bedroom. Joe sat and watched with his hands over his ears. He was tired of Beth's silly song. She was only four. To her, everything was a game.

"Come on, Joe," said his dad in a grumpy voice. "You're supposed to be packing your toys – not daydreaming!"

Joe sighed. He kicked one of the boxes with his trainer – but softly, so his dad didn't see. Then he slowly began to fill up the box.

Before Joe went to sleep, his dad came to say Goodnight. He looked at all the neatly packed boxes and smiled.

"Well done, Joe," he said. "This is the worst part of moving, all this packing. Just wait until we get to the new place! You'll have a big garden to play in – and a room of your own. You'll love it!"

Joe just nodded. When his dad had gone, he lay listening to his sister's breathing. After a while, he sat up in bed. He pulled back the curtains and looked at the yard outside. He could see his old sandpit up against the broken wall. And the patch of ground where he'd done his first head-stand. Binkie their cat sat washing herself on the step.

"I don't want to leave this place," thought Joe. "I like it here." He wriggled down under the duvet and pressed his face into the pillow.

The next morning, Joe sat on the step outside. Binkie was stretched out beside him in the sunshine. He rubbed her behind the ear.

Joe's mum sat down next to them. "I wonder what Binkie will think of the new place?" she said. "It will be really strange for her at first. She's lived here all her life."

"Just like me," said Joe.

"Mmm," his mum went on. "Everything will smell different, won't it? And the garden will seem huge. I wonder if she'll be scared?"

Joe thought about it. "I could help her," he said. "I could hold her and show her round. She wouldn't be frightened then, would she?"

Joe's mum gave him a big smile. "That's a great idea!" she said. "We'll put you in charge of Binkie. Thanks, Joe."

Soon it was Moving Day. Joe and Binkie sat in the empty bedroom. Through the window, they watched the removal people carrying boxes. Everything was loaded into a huge van.

"Goodbye bedroom," said Joe sadly.

Just then, Joe's mum came in with a cat box. "Let's put Binkie in here now," she said, "then she'll be safe in the car. You can hold her box on your lap."

Joe and his mum lifted Binkie into the cat box. And Joe carefully carried her out to the car.

At the new house, Beth went straight into the garden. Soon she was running about in the bushes, waving a stick.

Joe took Binkie into a quiet room and let her out of the cat box. Binkie sniffed around for ages. Then she followed him into his new bedroom. He tried to plan where all his things would go. He went to the window and looked out at the big, overgrown garden. Beth and his mum waved to him. Joe smiled.

Two days later, Joe and Binkie were in the garden. They'd discovered a pond with four tiny frogs. Binkie jumped at a butterfly in the long grass. Joe thought he'd make a den here, by the fence.

Joe's mum came along the path and crouched down beside them.

"Do you think Binkie likes it here?" she asked.

"You bet she does," replied Joe " – just like me!"

Dear Christopher

I'm sad without you. Nothing is the same. It's so quiet next door in your old house. The new lady hasn't got any children. We don't see her much. I miss playing with you after tea. I just sort of hang around. I wish the school holidays were over.

Here are some paper planes. I hope they don't get squashed in the post. I wish we could come to live next to you in your new house. Mum says we can't. But I can come over at half-term to stay, if that's OK with your mum. We can play that monster Lego game. I can bring my bike.

See you

Jamie

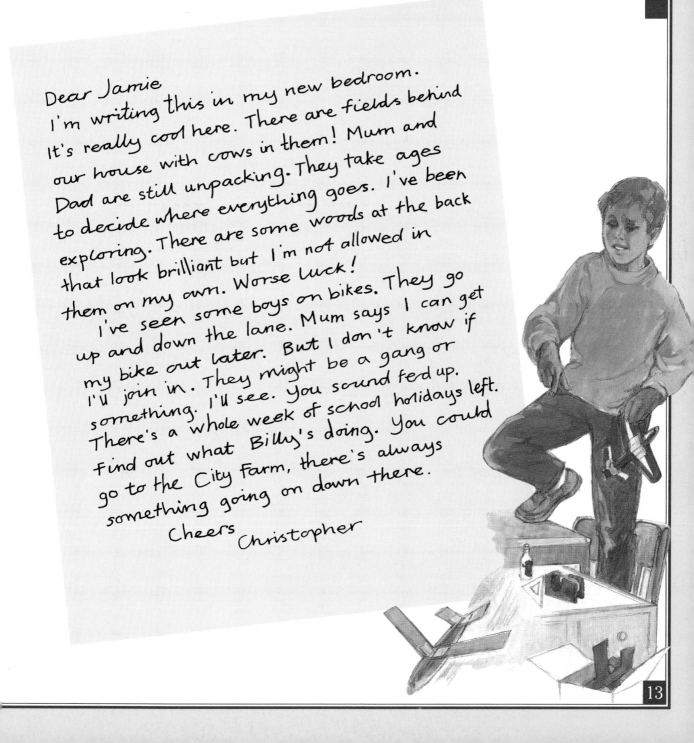

Dear Jamie

I'm writing this in my new bedroom. It's really cool here. There are fields behind our house with cows in them! Mum and Dad are still unpacking. They take ages to decide where everything goes. I've been exploring. There are some woods at the back that look brilliant but I'm not allowed in them on my own. Worse luck!

I've seen some boys on bikes. They go up and down the lane. Mum says I can get my bike out later. But I don't know if I'll join in. They might be a gang or something. I'll see. You sound fed up. There's a whole week of school holidays left. Find out what Billy's doing. You could go to the City Farm, there's always something going on down there.

Cheers
Christopher

13

FEELINGS: WHAT WILL HAPPEN?

When you first hear that you are moving to a new home you may have lots of questions. How far away will you be going? Will you need to change schools? What will your new home be like?

■ For many children this is an exciting time. It may be a bit worrying, too. Some children worry that they may not like the new place as much as their old home. It's hard to imagine living somewhere you don't know. Will there be the same things to do?

Kim worries that she won't be able to go to Art Club when she moves.

■ Many children feel concerned about fitting in somewhere new. They wonder who they will play with and how they will make friends. The thought of a new

school worries lots of children. They wonder if the work will be the same as they are used to. What will the teachers be like?

■ Many children want to know exactly when they will be moving. And their parents find it hard to give an exact date – there may be lots to sort out. This may make the children feel unsettled.

■ Some childen who are moving simply feel sad. Like Kim, they think of the friends they are leaving. For some, this crowds out every other thought.

■ It can be a sad time for those left behind, too. If your best friend is moving away, it can feel like the end of the world for you.

■ It's also a difficult time for parents. There will be a lot of extra work for them. They may seem always busy and impatient. Don't forget, they may be feeling a bit sad too. They will be leaving behind their own friends and the place they know.

LEFT BEHIND

If your best friend is moving away you could make a moving-in present to give them. Fix a time to see them – then you will both have that time to look forward to! If you saw your friend every day at a certain time, plan what you'll do then instead. You might ask another friend round to play, visit someone else, or learn to do something new. Talk about it with your mum or dad.

15

GETTING READY TO MOVE

If you're feeling sad and confused about moving, don't keep it to yourself. Talk to your mum or dad or another adult you trust. There are some other ways you can help yourself too.

■ Find out as much as you can about what is going on. If there's anything practical you are concerned about – such as if you will finish off the term at your old school or where you will be sleeping in the new house – then ask.

■ Ask if you may visit the new place. If not, is there a photograph you could look at? See if you can visit your new school. Look on the noticeboard and find out about after school clubs and other activities.

■ Plan how you'll set out your new room. If you'll be sharing a room, think about how you'll arrange it together.

- Before the move, try to pack up your own things. Then you'll feel in charge. Write your name on the boxes or mark them with stickers. You could leave out one or two special toys and put them in a backpack. Carry this with you on Moving Day.

- Ask what you can do to help on Moving Day. Like Joe in the story, you might be in charge of the family pet or a younger brother or sister. Talk about it with your parents first.

- Fix up a date for your best friend to visit you in your new home. (Check with your parents first.) Plan to write to your friends. Ask if you may telephone them, too, sometimes.

- Remember, you will make new friends in your new home. We make friends everywhere we go in life. Our number of friends just keeps on growing.

Dear Gran
This is your first letter from our new house! I've just finished unpacking all my things. It took two whole days. The first night here was weird. It was hard to get to sleep. There were all sorts of strange noises. Mum said it was the central heating. I don't think I'll ever find my way around here. All the streets look exactly the same.

I haven't started my new school yet but I've been to visit. One girl in my class was really friendly. Her name is Ellie.

Kayleigh's coming to stay next weekend. Mum says you are coming soon. I can't wait to show you everything. These are the things I like about here — my room, the street (but there are no trees), the park, Ellie at school, the kitchen (but it's full of boxes). Things I miss — Kayleigh, our old garden, Art Club, my old school, my teacher. See you soon.

Love Kim

Dear Kim

Thankyou for your letter. I'm really looking forward to my visit.

I'm glad that the move went well. It will take some time for you all to settle in. I remember it took me a while to feel that this was my home, and I only moved from two streets away! Once you've started at school, you'll soon get to know people. I think you need to do lots of things in your house to make it feel yours. How about having some schoolfriends home to tea?

Why don't you make a map of your new neighbourhood? Ask Mum or Dad to go for a walk with you at the weekend. Make a note of all the landmarks as you go along — shops, post boxes, traffic lights, churches, trees. When you get home, draw it out on a big sheet of paper. That will help you learn your way around. It will also help me not to get lost when I come to stay!

Love Gran

FEELINGS: IN A NEW PLACE

For many children, learning to enjoy a new place takes hardly any time. They find they've made themselves at home almost straight away. For others, settling in takes longer.

■ Some children hate the feeling of being new. They don't know what to do with themselves after school. They aren't sure of their way around. They stay at home a lot. This may make them feel lonely or bored.

■ Other children feel worried about what each new day will bring. They take it out on people at home. They snap at others or become moody.

■ Some children take longer to fit into school. They keep thinking of the way they used to do things. Everything in the new school seems different and confusing.

■ Some children find it hard to make new friends. They worry about what others are thinking of them. They feel shy and left out.

■ Many children who have moved feel extra tired at the end of the day. Remembering new names and places is tiring for anyone. It's a good idea to get plenty of rest.

■ If you feel any of these things, don't worry. They are all part of being new. Do try telling someone – a parent or another adult you trust. It would help to tell your teacher too. He or she may have some other ideas for helping you to settle in.

■ Remember that life changes all the time. And mostly change brings new and good things.

PETS ON THE MOVE

Moving home can be a confusing time for your pet, too. Everywhere looks and smells different. If you have a cat, keep it in for the first few days. Introduce your pet to one room first, let it sniff around and feel safe. Slowly let it explore the whole house. Always feed your pet in the same place. Just like people, some animals take longer than others to settle in. Give them time – and plenty of affection.

GETTING ON WITH YOUR NEW LIFE

If you are finding it a struggle to settle in to life in the new place, it might help to remember these things:

■ Learning the way around your new area will give you confidence. Look at a map and talk it through with a grown-up. Make your own map, as Kim's gran suggested.

■ Never be afraid to ask. If there's something you don't understand at your new school – like a new way of doing things, or where a room is – ask someone.

■ If you're feeling lonely and left out, think what you can do to change things. Make a list of all the places you could go to meet others – gym club, the sports centre, swimming club, the park. Ask an adult to help you. Is there anyone at school you'd like to invite home for tea?

- Other people don't know what you're thinking. If you stand back from the crowd, people may not realise that you're just feeling shy. They may think you are unfriendly. Be brave and greet people with a smile! It may seem hard at first – but practice helps.

- Give yourself time. It takes a while to get to know new people. Try not to be too upset if one group doesn't seem friendly. Keep trying. There's someone out there who would love to be your friend.

Making Friends

Here are some ideas to help when you're feeling shy. Think about the other person. Try to forget about yourself – just for a moment. Smile and say Hello. (Your heart might beat faster and you might go red. Try not to worry – it's normal to feel like this sometimes.) Ask the other person a question about themselves. This shows the other person that you care. And you'll learn something about them.

23

ALICE'S NEW SCHOOL

Alice tried to eat the toast in front of her. It was cold now, and the butter had made it soggy. Her throat was dry and she had to keep swallowing.

"All ready?" asked Alice's mum, coming into the kitchen. "We'd better set off soon. We don't want to be late on your first day!"

Alice pushed her chair back from the table and ran to clean her teeth. Her heart started to thump in her chest.

Soon Alice was strapping on her helmet and wheeling her bike on to the road. She could feel her heart beating faster. Alice was nervous. It was her first day in her new school.

Alice cycled close behind her mum and looked around. She liked the look of their new town. The pavements were wide and there were plenty of trees.

Soon the streets filled with children. They walked in groups or in pairs, laughing and talking together.

"I wonder if any of those girls will be in my class?" thought Alice.

"I'll wait and see you into school," said Alice's mum at the gates.

"OK," nodded Alice, gratefully.

In the classroom, Mrs Michael the teacher introduced Alice to the class. There was a new boy, too, called Tom.

"I'm sure everyone's keen to get to know you both," said Mrs Michael, smiling.

Alice went bright red and looked at her feet.

It was the start of a new term. Mrs Michael handed out books and explained where everything was. Alice tried to concentrate but she wasn't really listening.

"What will happen at break?" she wondered, panicking. "Who will I talk to? What shall I do?"

At last break came. The class rushed out into the playground. Tom ran off with some boys for a game of football. Alice leaned against the wall. She wished she could go home right now.

A group of girls came by. Alice recognised them from her class. They smiled at Alice. The tallest girl, Sue, said Hello. But Alice couldn't say a word. She nodded and put her head down.

The girls walked away. Alice stayed leaning against the wall. She pretended she didn't care. But inside she wanted to cry.

Sue and the others started running about. They were playing some kind of chase. Alice watched them out of the corner of her eye.

Just then, Sue ran headfirst into the wall. Bang! She fell down on the ground and lay still. The others stopped. They stood and stared. Everyone waited for Mrs Michael to arrive.

Alice could see Sue's bag open on the ground. Without thinking, Alice picked it up and dashed over to Sue.

"It's not too bad," Mrs Michael was saying in a calm voice. "I expect it was a shock, though."

Mrs Michael looked up and saw Alice.

"Ah, thank you, Alice," she said. "Now please hold Sue's hand a moment while I go and get the First Aid Box."

Alice sat down next to Sue. They talked about what had happened until Mrs Michael came back.

After a rest in the headteacher's room, Sue joined the others in class. She smiled across at Alice and Alice smiled back.

At lunchtime, Alice, Sue, Karen and Kate sat together.

"We thought you were really stuck up at first," said Karen.

Sue nodded. "You wouldn't look at us or say Hello."

"I was shy, that's all," explained Alice. "It's hard being new."

"Well, you're not new anymore," said Sue, laughing. "It feels as if I've known you for ever."

And Alice knew exactly what she meant.

Dear Christopher,

We've got Mrs. Fielding this term—she's great. We're doing special projects about where we live and what it used to be like hundreds of years ago. What's your new school like?

I go around with Josh and Kieran now. We go to the park after tea - you know the part where we made a den? It's Kieran's birthday on Saturday. He's having a swimming party with pizzas afterwards at his house. It'll be great. There's a new boy Joe in class this year. He's O.K. I'm going to tea with him on Wednesday. We do judo after school on Wednesdays. I told you I was starting. Do they have judo at your school? See you in two weeks (that's half-term).

Jamie

Dear Jamie

I'ts great here. You wait till you see it! We go out on our bikes every day. There's a boy Sam and he's got a big brother called Patrick. At the weekend we pack up sandwiches for lunch. We eat them in the field like a picnic. We can do it when you come.

I like school too. Our teacher is Mr Nicol. He's got a beard and glasses and a booming voice but he's a real joker. We have more homework than at Westley Park but it's O.K. We aren't allowed to play football in the playground here because someone smashed a window last term. We have to go down on the green. It gets all muddy when it rains and we get filthy - Dad goes mad! We don't have judo at our school but I go swimming on Thursdays. See you next week. Bring your bike!

Cheers! Christopher

31

HELPLINES

If you are feeling really worried and alone, you could telephone or write to one of these offices. Sometimes the telephone lines are busy. If they are, don't give up. Try them again.

ChildLine
Freephone 0800 1111
Address ChildLine Freepost 1111
London N1 0BR

The Samaritans
Telephone 0345 909090